Kingdom of Benin

Short stories

Ehi Edo Warrior chief

and

Uki at Ukpe Festival

Ehi Edo Warrior Chief
Kingdom of Benin stories

Website: www.kingdomofbenin.weebly.com
Enquiries and contact: fidelianimmons@gmail.com

Contents

'Just as the sun and the moon always reach their destinations and return safely the next day, so will may you go and come back safely to us.'

Forward

Ehi Edo Warrior Chief is a historical fiction story based on facts of war tactics employed by the Great Kingdom of Benin military. The Oba, who was the commander-in-chief of the military, supported by his high ranking officials and chiefs led and trained the army to the highest standards. Through this leadership and discipline, Great Kingdom of Benin army rose to become the superior power on the West African coast and remained so for centuries until the British and colonisation era (1200AD to 1897AD).

In this story, a neighbouring king asks for the assistance of Benin army to regain his country's independence from an occupying force. The story explores how the king is able to summon a large force of warriors in a day and the tactics they use to defeat the invaders. Through the main character Ehi, the story delves into the degree of skills and ambitions of individual soldiers and the loyalty warriors had to their king and country and ways in which the king rewarded them.

Events in parts of this story may sound mythical, however we know from records and accounts of British troops' experiences during the 'Benin Massacre' and the subsequent Punitive Expedition of 1897 that Benin warriors operated in this way; these records by the British correspond to oral accounts of Benin war tactics narrated over time by Kingdom of Benin elders. Captain Bacon recorded in his scrapbook written in 1897 (*BENIN – THE CITY OF BLOOD BY COMMANDER R.*

H. BACON, R. N. Intelligence Officer to the expedition, 1897) that the British soldiers could not see any Benin soldier on the battle field but they could hear them and that the first time they saw a Benin soldier was when they arrived in the city. Benin elders tell the same story of how their warriors fought.

Stranger than fiction one may say, but the Benin army was well advanced of their European counterparts in warfare during the medieval period and before the advent of the maxim machine gun which was used to defeat them in 1897. We know the effects of this to be equivalent to the nuclear weapon used against Hiroshima in 1945 and which brought about the end of World War II.

It is fair to attest that Benin soldiers had a good standing in their time. They should therefore be remembered for this.

Ehi hurried along the footpath, keen to get to the palace as quickly as his legs could carry him; his majesty the king had sent word for a meeting at the crack of dawn the night before.

As he walked, his mind danced over many thoughts; what could his majesty want to discuss so early in the morning; he knew from experience that this could be one of a dozen subjects; could it be that the young princess Osuyi had finally managed to elope with her lover. That wayward girl has given the council a run for its money, for she has tried once or twice to run away and had been returned to the palace after border guards apprehended her. If indeed, the princess had run away, the matter could be decided swiftly, they would have to send a delegation to fetch her back and fine the young man's family bundles of yam and some kegs of palm wine for allowing this to happen. If that was the only case to be debated this morning, he should surely be back home before the sun starts to rise and have enough time to visit one of his farms before he begins his council duties for the day.

Ehi wondered about other reasons, perhaps a spy had been captured during the night or better still, a neighbouring king had sent word about not paying his annual tribute; if this were it, Ehi enjoyed nothing more than convincing an errant king to pay up or expect stiff penalties; he quite looked forward to these instances. His mind went to the last king they had to have a word with about this; how white the king's face had turned when they had given him his majesty's message that one of the chiefs could appear anytime and anywhere in his kingdom and that they could not be held responsible for events after that. This trick worked, time and time again, Edo chiefs had quite built a reputation for themselves, for which they were both feared and respected by all far and near; it was, after all quite a feat of accomplishment to be able to remain invisible in a crowd. Anyhow, Ehi knew he would find out the reason his majesty had summoned them soon enough.

As Ehi drew near the palace entrance, he noticed that nothing stirred and no one seemed about. He strode with urgency through the palace entrance porch, down the long corridor and into the council chambers where the chiefs gather during such summons from his majesty or when they had a state matter to discuss. Three other chiefs had already arrived and were sitting silently looking pensive. Chiefs Enoghasie, Osagie and Osazuwa did not as much as acknowledge his entrance; Ehi knew then that this must be a serious matter, he knew not to ask questions but take his seat and wait for the others to arrive.

When thirty six chiefs had arrived and taken their seats, Chief Enoghasie the most senior chief, checked that they had enough chiefs for a quorum. This was the number required by law to decide on important matters such as security of the kingdom; he beckoned to Ogun, his majesty's chief attendant to fetch his majesty.

'Oba ghato, Okpere.' Chief Enoghasie saluted the king as he entered the council chambers, simultaneously beating his left fist against his chest.

'Ise!' the other chiefs responded, also beating their left fists against their chests.

As his majesty sat down, his attendants immediately stood to attention at his side. 'Hmm;' His Majesty began; 'Idu has to be dealt with.'

'Idu, is that like the king of Idu?' Osazuwa, the most senior chief present asked.

'I am afraid so. Yes, the king of Idu, it seems he is planning to invade and occupy Konga.' His Majesty informed his chiefs: 'I received word last night that he is planning to replace their administration with his own.'

'He can't do that; Konga is ours, is it not?' Chief Osazuwa seemed visibly irritated.

'Our friend the king has therefore, sent an urgent message for assistance to repel this aggression.' His Majesty continued.

'Some people never learn; when is he planning this invasion?' Chief Osazuwa enquired.

'The information I have is that his army is on their way to Konga borders as we speak; Konga has not got enough skilled or trained soldiers to hold them up for a day; our friend begs for urgent assistance from us.'

The chiefs knew exactly what this meant, they would have to gather and prepare over twenty thousand soldiers for war by midday. There was no time to lose, word had to be sent to all warriors immediately, otherwise some may have left home for their day's jobs before news gets round to their houses. Konga was a good two days journey through the forest and this could be even longer if the bushes were thick and needed to be hacked through.

'Could the soldiers make Konga in less than two days?' His Majesty asked the council.

'If they walked fast and approached it from the north instead of the west, there is a possibility that they could manage one and a half days.' It was Ehi.

'What does everybody else think; do we leave right away, approaching Konga from the north or do we need some more time to sleep on this idea?' His Majesty was saying: 'for my view, I think if soldiers are summoned right away before they start going about their day's chores, they could leave by mid day then we stand a chance of being able to send Idu packing from Konga in less than one day?'

'We should act on that idea straight away.' Iyase the prime minister suggested.

'Here, here.' the other chiefs agreed.

'Your majesty, we can summon five thousand soldiers right away, a further fifteen thousand will be able to join in about two hours.' Iyase informed the council.

'That is fine, those who arrive early can begin to get all they will need for the battle ready, so that by the time the others arrive, it will be just last minute skills practise that will be necessary.' Chief Osazuwa added.

'We are all agreed then; Iyase, send word to the soldiers, beat the drum, send runners, I want everyone in the courtyard in an hour.' His Majesty got up to leave the council chambers. The chiefs saluted him again:

'Oba ghato, Okpere'

'Ise!'

Iyase the prime minister set to work immediately, sending palace attendants with words to runners and drum beaters and clear messages to soldiers and their wives.

When the messages had been sent, he turned his attention to making the courtyard ready. The soldiers would need a clear space for a quick practise of their archery skills and enough room to hold twenty thousand soldiers, whilst his majesty, his chief priest and he inspected each one of them in turn to test their readiness for war. In the past a soldier had not remembered where his armlet should stay on his arm and remained visible for the enemy to see him and attack him; this should never happen to a Benin soldier; it was Iyase's responsibility to ensure that this never happened again.

'Ugie, see to it that the shields, the umozos, the asoros, the uhanbos, the ifenwes and the ekpedes have all been made ready.' Ugie was the King's chief priest, it was his job to ensure that all war weapons have been sharpened and poisoned ready to be used to deadly effect at a moment's notice.

Ugie had a team of priests who worked under him at the palace, he had already sent word to them and they had begun to arrive. As the priests arrived, they go to the king's storerooms of war arsenal to collect weapons they would need and begin to work on them.

Soon all the war weapons have been made ready and as the soldiers arrive, they submit their personal weapons to the priests to be made ready, spears and arrowheads needed fresh poison applied to them. Within the hour, the palace courtyard was half full of soldiers and military hornblowers, all excitedly anticipating their mission.

'Oba ghato, Okpere'

'Ise!'

His majesty had just come into the courtyard.

All the warriors stand to attention in their divisions to be inspected.

'Chiefs, have you got your five hundred men and counted that you have equal balance of archers, spearmen, crossbowmen and swordsmen?' Iyase asked.

'Eh!' They confirmed.

'Ehi, come out here.' His Majesty called.

In an instant, Ehi was out.

'Okay Chiefs, here is your model, check that you have all the kits that Ehi here, has;' His Majesty commanded; 'Ehi, show everyone what you have.'

Ehi proudly stepped forward, pleased to be chosen for the demonstration exercise to others; though deep in his heart, he knew it was a only a reminder and that other chiefs were as good as him and some even more accomplished; all the same this was his moment and he was going to make the most of it.

'First and foremost I have my shield and the correct way to use this is;' Ehi got on his knees and placed the shield in front of him. The shield covered him completely; 'I can place it in any direction the enemy is firing from; as you can see I am completely covered and no spear or arrow can penetrate my shield and get at any part of my body.'

Ehi then showed them his helmet and correct placement on his head; 'As you can see, my helmet made from hard crocodile skin and wood cannot be penetrated by spears of arrows.' He then twirled around to show them his body armour; this consisted of a top and a bottom reaching to his knees and made from quilted wool and strengthened crocodile skin. All war chiefs and highly decorated soldiers wore these war dresses in all battles and wars.

'As you know, if the leader falls, the battalion falls too. Can you all check that there is no damage to any of your weapons and body armour!' His Majesty commanded.

Satisfied with the chiefs, he turned his attention to the other warriors.

'Chiefs check your warriors' kits now; inspect their shields and body armours, you should all be able to arrive safely back home without a single a scratch on your body;' His Majesty continued to pray aloud; 'for just as the sun and the moon always reach their destinations and return safely the next day, so will you all go and come back to us.'

'Ise!' the whole courtyard echoed.

Iyase and Ugie had also began to inspect the warriors; looking into their protection charms calabashes and feeling them to check that they have been attached firmly to their war dresses. This was only as a precaution, for they knew that no Edo warrior would take any chances with being caught off guard by the enemy and that every single one of them would have daily checked his war dress and equipment, ready for the call from His Majesty.

'Check where you have placed that armlet on your arm;' Ugie told Eboyi, a young soldier, 'you really do not want to be invisible just yet.'

'No sir, I don't. ' Eboyi thanked Ugie; 'Thank you sir.'

'Good job everyone, it seems you are ready to depart, tie your egogo on now please;' Iyase advised the warriors; ' You want to intimidate the enemy before they even see you; you will find that, that is half the battle won, when you are feared without lifting a finger.'

By now, the courtyard was almost full; about fifteen thousand soldiers were present and ready for action.

'We will send the other five thousand soldiers by the time the sun starts to go down, so that by tonight you will have twenty thousand ready for action in the morning. Good luck and the gods Osun and Ogun go with you; we will carry on praying for you here.' Iyase blessed the soldiers.

'Send word as soon as you have secured Konga;' His Majesty reminded them; 'do not forget that you are sons of Osun and Ogun and that they are with you right now and will protect you throughout this mission; go safely and return soon.'

After this blessing, His Majesty left the courtyard.

'Oba ghato, Okpere'

'Ise!' The courtyard echoed again.

Iyase and Ugie remained behind to see the warriors off safely.

With these prayers, blessings and encouraging words from his majesty, the warriors felt very courageous about this mission for they had just been blessed by Osanobua himself, they knew that all would be well.

'Ehi, you are in charge of this mission.' Iyase revealed.

Though taken by surprise, Ehi was delighted with this faith placed in him and vowed to himself, there and then to lead the soldiers to the best of his ability; he would not lose a single one of them.

Iyase commanded the drum beat for their exit and the commanding chiefs began to move their battalion out of the palace holding courtyard, through a secret passage way from the palace into the deep jungle for their mission ahead. Ehi was the first to depart for he knew the forest like the back of his hand and had been to Konga through the north several times; he could shorten their journey time using the shortcuts he knew well. He was also their leader for this mission.

The warriors were in high spirits and not wanting to lose any time before getting to their destination, most declined the offer to stop for food on the way; those who wanted subsistence picked from the variety of succulent fruits on offer from the forest, eating as they travelled.

At dusk, they came to a clearing; on hearing the sound of flowing water, Ehi decided it was a good spot to camp for the night and wait for the others to catch up. His Majesty had promised that five thousand more warriors would join them by the end of the day. Ehi had left clear instructions with Iyase on the direction they should take to find the path they were travelling through. The warriors will be able to find this and follow them using the clues from the smell and sight of freshly cut wood branches. Ehi's men have had to hack their way through thick forest growth to make a short cut path to Konga borders; the warriors behind will know to follow this path.

Soon the other chiefs and warriors joined them; Ehi consulted the other chiefs on whether they should camp or carry on; 'We may as well camp here;'

Chief Osazuwa agreed; 'there seems plenty of food here too; ask the men to find a spot to pitch for the night.'

After the warriors had all settled down, it was time for them to look for food. As good farmers and hunters, the camp was soon awash with all manner of fresh fruit, vegetable and game. There was plantain, bananas, corn, yams, sweet potatoes, efo, peas, pawpaw, mango, rabbits, deer and some delicacies like woodworm. It was feasting before fighting time. Ehi and Chief Osazuwa reminded the warriors to leave enough food for the other warriors joining them later. Sure enough, before the sun went down, over five thousand new warriors joined the camp. All were ready for action the next day.

At the first sight of day light, Ehi was up, stirred a hornblower to awaken the others and went to a quiet spot to use the sun rise position to work out the north direction. Soon he was joined by Chief Osazuwa; 'Which direction are we going in next?' he asked; Ehi pointed to the right; 'We better get the men ready.'

When they returned back to camp, the warriors were all already awake and getting ready.

'Okay, everyone gather around!' Ehi called. Soon every warrior had congregated around Ehi and Chief Osazuwa for last minute briefing.

'Take this opportunity to top up your water supply; eat as much as you can, for I do not think that we will have another morsel to eat till our mission is accomplished later today. I reckon Konga is about half a day's journey away, so we should still be refreshed by then.' Ehi informed the warriors; 'we will decamp in an hour, everyone should have checked their weapons and be fully dressed by then; off you go.'

Soon the camp was a beehive of activities, warriors fetching water from the nearby river, some eating and some clearing the camp.

This last stage of the journey was very important for the military hornblowers; they had the vital job of creating an aura of invincibility around the warriors. The blasts from their horns which sounded like thousands of hurricanes could be heard for miles around. The enemy on hearing these coupled with the clanging sounds of the egogos worn by the warriors, were terrified into submission; only a few foolish ones, thinking themselves brave, have ever dared to put up a fight.

'Okay, sound the horn.' Ehi instructed his battalion head hornblower. Soon all the chiefs and their battalions were ready.

'Put your egogos on and we are ready to depart.' Chief Osazuwa added.

'We are travelling in that direction;' Ehi was saying, pointing to the right; 'your commanding chief, will give the signal for you to tighten your armlet when the enemy is in sight; remember that you do not do so before that order.'

'If possible capture the enemy alive, we do not kill others unless our life is in danger, we acknowledge that it is a blessing from Osanobua to have all the skills we do, we will therefore not misuse them.' Chief Osazuwa was the eldest chief and it fell to him to give the last words of encouragement to the warriors and to bless them.

'Just as the sun and the moon always reach their destinations and return safely the next day, so will we all go and come back safely.' He prayed.

'Ise!' all the warriors responded.

Ehi led the way towards Konga; they travelled light this time as they did not need to carry food, this quickened their pace and so they made Konga borders earlier than they had anticipated. On signal from Ehi, his battalion warriors tightened their armlets around their upper arms; this had the effect of creating an instant invisibility circle around them. No one else could see them when their armlets were worn and tightened on the upper part of their arms; this gave them the advantage of surprise attack on their enemies.

Moving stealthily, soon Ehi and his men were inside Konga borders, where they surrounded Idu soldiers. As some of them were disarmed, others tried in vain to fight back at an enemy they could not see, whilst a few of them beat their drums to warn that Edo soldiers had arrived. As their reinforcement soldiers arrived, they were disarmed by the Edo warriors.

'Quick, make a retreat; it is an ambush from Edo soldiers.' a soldier who looked like he was a commanding chief advised. It was no use Idu soldiers had been completely surrounded and in this state, they surrendered.

At this, Ehi gave signal for the warriors to loosen their armlets and they became visible and could be seen again.

At this sight, Idu soldiers fell to the ground, begging for mercy.

'Who is in charge here?' Ehi asked?

'I am.' One of the Idu soldiers replied.

'Well then, take your men, go back to your king and tell him that Konga is not for the taking, it is an Edo territory.' Ehi warned; 'tell him we will not be this lenient next time, do you understand?

Chief Osazuwa came closer to assist Ehi, two Edo commanding chiefs looked a formidable sight and gave the message that a swifter response was required.

'Yes.' murmured the soldier.

'We did not quite hear that, say it out loud so that all Konga people can hear you say it and be the witnesses to your word, this day.'

'Yes!' The soldier shouted.

'Off with you and take every single one of your men.' Ehi ordered the soldier.

'We will have to supervise their departure to ensure that no one of them lurks around.' Chief Osazuwa pointed out. However the Idu soldiers had received such a shock, that no one of them was prepared to hang around to see what the Edo warriors might do next; they fled as fast as they could and in their haste left some of their effects behind. The battle was over by early evening.

Word reached King of Konga, who had gone into hiding when Idu soldiers invaded his land that Edo soldiers had arrived and sent his enemy packing. He felt safe enough to come out of hiding, knowing that Idu soldiers would never bother him again and knowing that he could get Edo soldiers out in less than five days. Heading for his palace, he sent word to all the households in his domain to prepare a bed for the night for the Edo soldiers, who he knew would not want to be travelling back during the night. He wanted to show them some appreciation and hospitality.

By the time he arrived at his palace, the Edo soldiers were resting in the large market square; his people had already began to give them food, water and palm wine. There was celebration all around.

Ehi and Chief Osazuwa went to consort with him about arrangement for their comfort tonight and to discuss future protection arrangements; they needed to take work back to his majesty back at home.

'Thank you my friends;' the king of Konga began; 'I do not know how I am going to repay you, I must send a young bride to your king and you must choose a damsel each for yourselves too. Any of your soldiers who need a wife can choose from our fine maidens.'

'That will not be necessary your majesty, we just need to know that you are satisfied with our work and that you will come and see his majesty soon.' Ehi explained.

'Of course, yes; say in four market days?'
King of Konga promised.

'That is that then, can you ask your
people to show every one of our soldiers
their beds for the night. We will set off
back home in the morning at first light
of day; we have many other
commitments back at home.' Ehi was
anxious to rest after the long day,
they've had; he wanted to be properly
prepared for their return journey back
home. After tonight's feasting, he hoped
that the warriors would be ready to
leave Konga in the morning and not
start getting spoilt with the
merrymaking. .

After their meeting with the king of
Konga, Ehi was taken to one of the
chiefs' houses to spend the night. He
was pleased to find that the chief had

already prepared presents for him to take back home but he wanted to travel light and gently declined the offer; 'Maybe you could send them to follow us;' he asked the chief to send the presents some other time, all he could think about right now was getting a good night's sleep and getting back to the palace with news for his majesty about how the mission was accomplished; there was also likely to be another mission waiting for them.

As he closed his eyes that night, Ehi dreamt about the community welcome celebrations that will be held for him and the other warriors back home. He wondered if his majesty would ask his bronze casters to set him in bronze forever; he hoped so with all his heart, for he would like all future generations to know about him and to see him smiling down at them from his bronze plaque, hanging up there on the palace walls.

Word Meanings

Oba: king

Iyase: Prime minister

'Oba ghato, Okpere': Long live the king

'Ise': Amen

Asoro: spear

Calabash: container made from the shell of gourd fruit

Efo: spinach

Egogo: quadrangular bell

Ekpede: crossbow

Ifenwe: arrow

Market days: One Edo week, comprising four days.

Ogun: god of iron and war

Osanobua: Almighty god

Osun: god of the forests, medicines and charms

Palm wine: an alcoholic drink made from the sap of some species of the palm tree

Uhanbo: bow

Umozo: sword

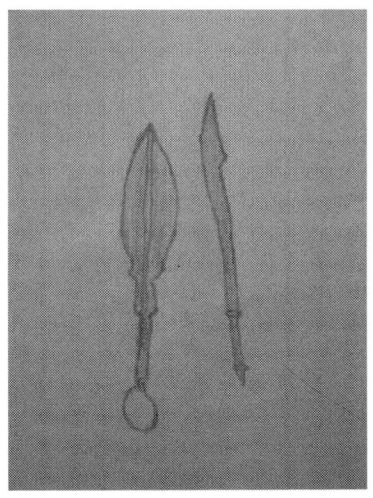

Uki at Ukpe Festival

Kingdom of Benin stories

Foreword

Kingdom of Benin people liked to have a good time; they took every opportunity to have fun.

We know from Benin bronzes plaques that the people engaged in many celebrations and festivals. In addition to the king's numerous festivals, his chiefs and other families had occasions to celebrate too; for example, chiefs held community celebrations to mark special events like their chieftaincy title conferment. Families too celebrated birth of an heir or of a special child. All those who could afford it, celebrated marriages and burial of family members; these were lavish occasions.

Uki at Ukpe Festival is one girl's contribution to the celebration of the

*New Year. During this time, the Oba
ushered in the New Year with a nine day
festival which included praying for good
fortune for his people and community.
The festival also included activities such
as feasting, dancing and masquerading.*

*Uki is part of a girls dance group, who
have to performance for the community
at the palace during Ukpe, the New Year
festival. She wants to look and perform
her best; her beads and braided hair all
add to her beauty at the performance.
Her family support her throughout her
practice and final performance.*

Uki, meaning *moon* was doing her best to concentrate on tonight's moonlight games but she was not having much luck, she was losing all about everyone one of them, which was unlike her. She was trying very hard to focus but this was proving very difficult, her mind on tomorrow's Ukpe festival and how she was going to perform, she was very excited about the dance.

Her name *Uki*, had been given to her by her grandfather because she was born on the day, the day and night were of equal length just after the harvest festival. Her people believed that the moon was the most important heavenly body because through the phases of the moon, they got their seasons; they named their months, counted their days and structured their nights when the

sun god had
gone to bed. To
her people, the
moon occupied a
very special
place in their
survival,
although, they did not worship the
moon as a god as they did the sun, the
God Osun.

To be named Uki was mega special for a
child, Uki sometimes felt like she made it
possible for all the other children to
delight themselves at night when she
(Uki) shone brightly in the sky.

Tonight though, Uki did not feel like
living up to her name, she could not wait
for the night to be over and the morning
to begin. Tomorrow she would make a
name for herself, she would become the

talk of the town; she just knew that she would.

'How long, till the cock crows?' Uki asked her sister Ewan, when the moon had finally gone down and they were in bed.

'A very long time.' was the reply.

'But how long, I need to know.' Uki pressed for an answer.

'Not very long, you just close your eyes and before you know it, the cock will crow.' Ewan reassured her sister. Uki closed her eyes and tried to sleep but she could not, her mind kept going back to her dance; she tossed from one side to the other and this carried on for what seemed like eternity.

'Cock-a-doo-doodle.'
It was the cock
crowing. Uki jumped
up barely able to
contain herself, she
could feel her heart
pounding; she ran to
the door, pushed it open and ran to the
centre of the courtyard where the water
barrel was. She filled her calabash up
with water and carried it to the back of
the girls' quarters where their bathroom
was. She scooped some water, poured it
over her body and reached for the soap
bowl to begin to wash herself but it was
empty. 'No soap;' she shouted 'someone
bring me some soap!' No one answered.
'Someone bring me some soap.' still no
reply; she knew then that she would
have to go and fetch some herself.

She put her wrap around her and went back into the courtyard; she darted across to her grandma's kitchen where she knew some newly made soap was available. She soon found some in a basket that looked like it was ready for market, as she dug in for a scoop; 'What do you think, you are doing, young lady?' it was her grandma; 'That soap is for sale at the market.' She said.

'But it is still in the pot, none of it is a bar yet.' Uki protested; 'so we can use it.'

'No you cannot; take some from the plate next to the fireplace.'

Uki was very proud of her grandma's reputation as the best soap maker around; she'd made lots of money from her soap sale, making her a very rich woman in the community. Uki knew better than to try to argue with her, her grandma knew all there was to know about black soap. She knew how to combine ash from the fire with red palm oil to make the smoothest, best smelling soap around. Her grandma also knew how to pick fluffy white cotton from the seeds to make thread and she knew how to weave the thread into cloth. Sometimes Uki spent hours just watching her on the spindle spinning thread into cloth. Maybe her grandma would show her how to weave cloth some day and she could get very rich too. Right now, she needed a bath so she could get ready for her big day.

Uki took extra care to wash every part of her body, she must be sparkly today. She even had the special bath towel her grandma wove for her last Ukpe; 'Take it with you when you sleepover at your friends' houses;' she had told her then and for Uki, today felt special too. Reaching out for the bath towel, Uki carefully wrapped it around her body, it felt cosy; leisurely, she gently patted herself dry.

Uki joined her sisters in the girls quarters of their compound, the compound was rectangular in shape and divided into girls' quarters, boys' quarter, wives' quarters and her dad's quarter; inside the compound was a square courtyard, in the middle of which were six big water barrels and plenty of space for the family's livestock. During community festivals, the courtyard was also used for large scale cooking of food for the community.

'Here is your chewing stick.' Ewan held out her bitterleaf stick.

'Thank you, big sister.' Uki collected the chewing stick from her sister and went outside into the courtyard to brush her teeth. She quite enjoyed brushing her teeth with the bitterleaf stick. Her grandma had told her that the bitterleaf plant contained medicinal juice which stopped teeth from decaying and took away bad breath. Uki chewed on the bark to get the foamy green sap which she would use to wash her teeth and mouth. She slowly crushed the wooden part to make a fine tooth brush. Using her newly made tooth brush and foamy sap, she cleaned her teeth till she felt a smooth sweet taste in her mouth; she knew then that her teeth were clean. To finish off, she rinsed her mouth out with some cold water and went back into the girls' quarters.

'Where is the body oil?' she asked Ewan.

'It is where you left it last night, with your skirt and beads.' Ewan was not being helpful; she was busy getting their breakfast ready and did not want to be disturbed. Uki remembered her stuff were in the bedroom next door. Rubbing gently, she oiled her olive skin till she was shiny all over. She loves this body oil, for it was made by her grandma from palm kernels which she roasted till all the oil came out; to this she added some fragrance. Uki could smell the sweet aroma on her body, she felt proud of her grandma's many skills. Putting on her skirt, beads and ankle rattles, she went to find someone to watch her practise her dance. As she walked, the rattles made a jingly sound which drew her mum and sisters' attention and they all came to watch her practise.

'Do you want to see my dance?' She smiled.

'Go on then, show us.' It was her grandma. Uki started to dance; 'Stop, where is your fan?' she asked.

'It is in the big bedroom;' her mum said; 'Ewan, go and get it for her.'

'I am not a slave you know.' Ewan protested.

'Please just go and get it; I will give you some money for it; thank you dear.' her mum begged; Ewan went to fetch the fan.

Uki moved so gracefully, they were all spellbound. 'You are truly beautiful, you dance like a spirit, everyone will love you today.' her grandma complimented.

'Of course, they will, she is Uki, the giver of the seasons.' Ewan sneered.

'Don't be a soar grape.' Uki whispered looking at her.

'I am not, I am praising you.' Ewan admired her sister's beauty. Uki felt as proud as a peacock and could not wait till many more people could see her dance; she would make sure that she stood out in her dance team. After her practise, she carefully took off her beads and ankle rattles, put them into her bag and went off to Ivie's house, where all the dancers have been instructed to meet.

When all twelve girls had arrived, Ivie's mum, gave them some breakfast consisting of roasted corn, pear and a selection of fruit; 'Make sure you have enough food inside you.' She advised them.

After practising and perfecting their song and dance moves for what seemed like most of the morning, they were ready for the day's performance at the palace.

'Let's make this the best Ukpe ever.' Edugie told them encouragingly.

'We will.' The girls replied in chorus, smiling at each other as they did so.

The crowd had quite gathered at the palace grounds when the girls arrived. Edugie their team leader asked them to follow her in a single file as she weaved her way through the crowd towards the centre of the palace square. She soon found a good spot. 'Wait here for me, I need to let Chief Omeike know that we have arrived.' and off she went in search of the chief who was one of the organisers of the Ukpe festival. The girls settled down to watch the masquerades who were performing; one of them was doing some daredevil somersaults which was getting the crowd roaring ecstatically. They were counting '48, 49, 50 ...' On this count, the troupe's leader ran after the masquerade, got hold of him and encircled him to stop him making any more moves. Everyone gave a big cheer. The masquerade staggered to a stop to more cheers from the crowd; they loved him.

A music band came into the centre of the palace square drumming, blowing horns, using shakers and other musical instruments to sing an ode to the king's reign. As they sang, a group of women in the crowd broke into the center of the square where the musicians were performing. They began to dance to their sweet song; soon everyone in the crowd was clapping rapturously. Finally: 'Zaiki!' it was Chief Omeiki signalling the end of the song; everyone chanted 'Zaiki!' His highness the king signalled his approval and everyone clapped. Uki wondered which was sweeter to say, 'Zaiki.' or 'Your highness.' she decided the former was,

as they both had the same meaning.
'Zaiki.' she said again.

The chief signalled to the girls that it
was almost their turn to perform.
Collecting their bags and walking in a
single file, they made for the palace
dressing rooms where they found a
vacant room. Here they dressed as
quickly as they could; they were soon
called to the holding area to wait to be
called. Uki grew nervous, she tried to
calm herself down by trying to
remember all the praises from her
sister, mum and grandma, but it was no
use, she was shaking all over. After what
seemed like ever, a palace attendant
came to collect them for their
performance. Edugie led the girls out in
a single file into the square where as
they entered, the crowd clapped and

cheered loudly; Uki could hear her sister Ewan, saying ' Uki, the giver of the seasons, shine brightly today.' This was all she needed, she soon forgot all about her fear and started to rock gently before she got into her position.

Edugie started to sing and on hearing her sweet voice, all the girls got into their position; on cue from her, they started their dancing; oh how the crowd roared. Edugie sang like the bird of the

air and the girls danced like water spirits and flamingos merged into one, the atmosphere was electric, the crowd threw coins at the dancers, they clapped, they cheered;

they almost
brought the sky
down with their
jubilation.

Amidst all the
cheering, Uki could
hear: 'Uki, Uki, Uki.' This was it; she'd
made it; one big cheer for Uki at the
Ukpe festival; 'Hooray!' She was now a
famous person; there will be no one to
top that today.

After their dance, it was feasting time,
Edugie led the girls back to her house
where cauldrons of food awaited them,
they had a good selection to chose from
including: white rice, jollof rice, mei-mei,
eba, ground rice, pounded yam, fruit,
selection of fried, baked or mashed
plantain, assortment of meat, goat, beef,
fish, snails and other delicacies. Uki and

the girls had the feast of their lives. 'Well done girls.' Edugie congratulated them; 'Eat up so we can go and continue watching the show.'

'You are coming to eat at my house at the next break.' Uki announced.

''Then it is at my house.' Ivie begged them; 'We can eat at other people's houses tomorrow, we still have three days of celebration left.'

Uki smiled, for as well as all the entertainment activities, she also liked all the feasting, wining and dining that go on during the Ukpe festival.

Kingdom of Benin Short Stories

Written by Fidelia Nimmons

Other story books by Fidelia Nimmons:

Dairy of An Edo Princess   £4.99

Ehi Edo Warrior Chief   £4.99

Books are available to purchase from Amazon.

Prices are subject to change.

Printed in Great Britain
by Amazon.co.uk, Ltd.,
Marston Gate.